NONFICTION COMPANION

TO

Christopher Paul Curtis's

Bud, Not Buddy

Lisa Kurkov

Rourke
Educational Media

BEFORE, DURING, AND AFTER READING ACTIVITIES

Before Reading: Building Background Knowledge and Academic Vocabulary

"Before Reading" strategies activate prior knowledge and set a purpose for reading. Before reading a book, it is important to tap into what your child or students already know about the topic. This will help them develop their vocabulary and increase their reading comprehension.

Questions and activities to build background knowledge:
1. Look at the cover of the book. What will this book be about?
2. What do you already know about the topic?
3. Let's study the Table of Contents. What will you learn about in the book's chapters?
4. What would you like to learn about this topic? Do you think you might learn about it from this book? Why or why not?

Building Academic Vocabulary
Building academic vocabulary is critical to understanding subject content.
Assist your child or students to gain meaning of the following vocabulary words.

Content Area Vocabulary
Read the list. What do these words mean?

- blacklisting
- emancipation
- Hooverville
- improvisation
- labor unions
- mortgages
- Morse code
- Pullman porter
- redlining
- Roaring Twenties
- scat
- stock market

During Reading: Writing Component

"During Reading" strategies help to make connections, monitor understanding, generate questions, and stay focused.
1. While reading, write in your reading journal any questions you have or anything you do understand.
2. After completing each chapter, write a summary of the chapter in your reading journal.
3. While reading, make connections with the text and write them in your reading journal.
    a) Text to Self – What does this remind me of in my life? What were my feelings when I read this?
    b) Text to Text – What does this remind me of in another book I've read? How is this different from other books I've read?
    c) Text to World – What does this remind me of in the real world? Have I heard about this before? (news, current events, school, etc.)

After Reading: Comprehension and Extension Activity

"After Reading" strategies provide an opportunity to summarize, question, reflect, discuss, and respond to text. After reading the book, work on the following questions with your child or students to check their level of reading comprehension and content mastery.
1. What was Bud's goal in the novel?
2. How does Bud feel at the end of the book?
3. How hard do you think it would be to travel like Bud did, today?
4. Have you traveled before? How did you get there? If you haven't, how would you like to travel?

Extension Activity
Bud, Not Buddy mentions labor unions, and this book goes more in-depth. Do your own research! Pick a labor union from the 1930s and learn more about it. Who was in it? What did they want? How did they protest?

TABLE OF CONTENTS

ABOUT *Bud, Not Buddy*

and **Christopher Paul Curtis**

The main character in *Bud, Not Buddy* is one who Christopher Paul Curtis dreamed up many years ago when he was working in a General Motors factory in Flint, Michigan. That character, Bud Caldwell, turned out to be a good one—Curtis won both the Newbery Medal and Coretta Scott King Award in 2000 for *Bud, Not Buddy*.

The novel, Curtis's second, tells the story of orphan Bud Caldwell, a young boy searching for his father in Depression-era Michigan. He encounters plenty of setbacks on his adventure, but his persistence and spirit, as well as the help of a few friends he meets along the way, guide him to a new family—even if it's not the one he was looking for.

Further Reading

Curtis's first book was The Watsons Go to Birmingham—1963. *Like* Bud, Not Buddy, *it is a work of historical fiction that is based, in part, on family experiences. The Watsons takes place during the civil rights movement —a turbulent time in American history. If you'd like to learn more, search* Watsons Go to Birmingham *and* trailer *on YouTube to see a preview of the movie based on the book.*

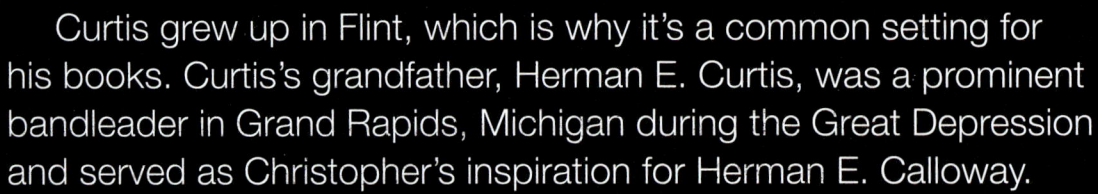

Curtis grew up in Flint, which is why it's a common setting for his books. Curtis's grandfather, Herman E. Curtis, was a prominent bandleader in Grand Rapids, Michigan during the Great Depression and served as Christopher's inspiration for Herman E. Calloway.

Like many writers, Curtis gets his inspiration from a variety of places. Some characters are based on people in his family or people he's met, while story ideas can come from anywhere—real events in history, things he's read, or conversations he's heard.

FLINT, MICHIGAN

From the Novel

Flint is the setting for the first half of Bud's story. Flint is where he's from (and all he's known) but he decides to travel to Grand Rapids to find his father.

Flint had a difficult time during the Great Depression. Unemployment rates in Michigan were about 8 percent higher than in the rest of the country. One reason for this was that the auto industry, a major employer in Michigan, didn't do well in the 1930s; no one could afford to buy a new car, so the factories had to lay off many people.

THE GREAT DEPRESSION

From the Novel

The novel takes place in 1936, right in the middle of the Great Depression, which lasted from 1929 to 1939. In addition to the fact that Bud is an orphan, the country's economy means it is harder than ever to find food, shelter, and clothing.

The Depression began in 1929 after the **stock market** crashed. Life changed overnight from the good times of the **Roaring Twenties**. Many people lost their jobs or had their hours and pay reduced. Suddenly, families had to cut back significantly. They mended clothing instead of buying new clothes. They planted gardens, preserved food, repaired old items, and reused household materials as much as possible.

Did You Know...

- *In 1933, one out of every four people was unemployed.*
- *The United States joined WWII only two years after the Depression ended.*
- *Bank closings resulted in more than a billion dollars in lost deposits.*
- *The "Black Brain Trust" was a group of African Americans who served as public policy advisors to President Franklin D. Roosevelt from 1933 to 1945.*
- *Marriage rates dropped by 22% during the Depression.*

Roosevelt

Americans cut back on leisure activities, like going to the movies or on vacation. Pastimes such as playing board games and mini-golf and listening to the radio were popular. Times were hard, so anything that could be a momentary distraction was welcome.

Before the Depression, many people looked down on welfare, or receiving monetary help from the government. That changed, however, when greater numbers of people started needing that help. Roosevelt's New Deal programs, like the WPA (Works Project Administration), were intended to create jobs for the unemployed and help them get by until times improved.

Before television, presidents would give addresses to the American people over radio.

Good Works

One of Roosevelt's most successful programs was called the Civilian Conservation Corps (CCC). Unemployed young men were paid to do environmental work. The CCC operated for about a decade, and in that time, planted more than 3 billion trees! The men fought forest fires, reseeded grazing land, and built wildlife refuges. They built trails and shelters in more than 800 parks—you may have even used one!

SOUP KITCHENS

From the Novel

Bud is saved from having to spend a day hungry by a family who pretends he belongs to them. Bud is late to get in line at the mission, and he knows that if he misses a free meal, he'll have to find food in the garbage or wait until dinner.

Although soup kitchens didn't serve only soup, it was a staple meal of the Depression. Soup is easy to make in large quantities. It's a simple way to use up leftovers, and it was easy to stretch by adding more water.

Early in the Depression, soup kitchens were privately funded by people or businesses who wanted to help the less fortunate. Later on, during Roosevelt's presidency, the government helped provide free meals to the needy.

Gangster Kitchen

One of history's most infamous soup kitchens was opened in Chicago, Illinois by the famous gangster and mob boss, Al Capone. Capone was known for violence and illegal activities of all kinds, but apparently, the idea of innocent people starving was more than he could stand. In 1930, Capone opened a soup kitchen that served more than 2,000 people a day!

HOOVERVILLES

From the Novel

Bud and Bugs look for food and a place to stay in "Hooperville," which is their misheard version of **Hooverville**. Just as they had hoped, they find a welcoming community willing to feed and shelter them in exchange for pitching in with daily duties.

Hoovervilles were shantytowns, or groupings of temporary homes made out of cardboard, wood, glass, tarpaper, tin, and cloth. They housed people who had been evicted from their homes and had nowhere else to go. The makeshift towns were named after President Herbert Hoover, who was regarded as having failed to help the American people in their greatest time of need.

Hooverisms

Hoovervilles weren't the only thing named after President Herbert Hoover. There are several other "Hooverisms" that came into use during the 1930s.

- *Hoover blankets = newspapers*
- *Hoover flags = inside-out and empty pockets*
- *Hoover hogs = squirrels, rabbits, and other rodents used for food*
- *Hoover shoes = worn-out shoes with cardboard for soles*
- *Hoover carts = carts patched together from broken-down automobiles and pulled by a mule or horse*

Hoovervilles varied in size from several hundred people to thousands in large cities. They were often located near rivers so that there would be a source of water. Some had vegetable patches. The largest Hooverville, located in St. Louis, Missouri, even had churches and an informal mayor!

The conditions in Hoovervilles were rough. People lived in cramped quarters, without bathrooms or running water. Residents became ill easily, and disease was quick to spread. The shantytowns were sometimes raided and broken up, as Bud experienced, but many people felt pity for those who lived there.

Giant Hooverville

One of the largest shanties was in Central Park. It was 20 feet tall! Stonemasons used stones from the nearby reservoir to build it. On the opposite end of the spectrum, the crudest shelters were inside large empty water pipes.

RIDING THE RAILS

From the Novel

Bud and his friend Bugs plan to ride the rails west to make money picking fruit. Bud doesn't make it onto the train, but Bugs does, which promptly ends their adventures together.

Riding the rails was a common but dangerous practice during the Depression. Men and boys (mostly) would illegally hop aboard trains. The riders often traveled west, looking for work or seeking adventure.

Conditions on the trains were far from ideal. They were dirty and unsanitary. Illness spread quickly. Food was hard to come by, and losing a limb was a definite possibility. Despite the risks, there were plenty of people who loved the freedom and exhilaration of riding the rails.

Bully Bulls

Railroad bulls were guards hired to stop people from riding the trains without paying. They were harsh, often beating or arresting homeless people who tried to evade them. The bulls threatened and stole from them, knowing that their actions were likely to go unpunished.

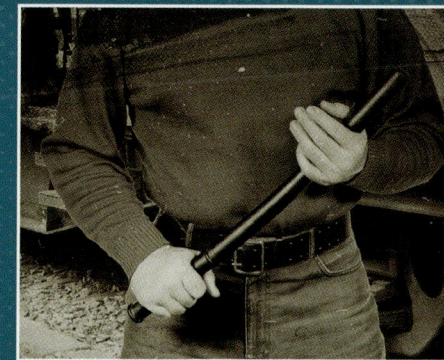

THE KKK

From the Novel

Before Lefty Lewis drops Bud off at the Log Cabin, he mentions that Bud shouldn't have been traveling across Michigan by himself at night. Lewis cautions him about the aggressive nature of the Ku Klux Klan in that area.

During the 1920s, a hate group called the Ku Klux Klan (KKK) became more powerful. The group grew in numbers and became more violent. Although today we often think of their hatred as targeting African Americans, they were also a danger to Catholics, Jews, and immigrant groups.

RACISM

Confederate Flag

This is the confederate flag. It was created in 1861 as one of many symbols for the Confederacy during the American civil war. However, in 1948 it became a symbol of opposition to the de-segregation movement in the U.S. It has continued to be used since then by groups like the KKK and other white nationalist organizations, as well as individuals, to symbolize racist ideals.

THE EMANCIPATION OF THE NEGROES, JANUARY, 1863—THE PAST AND THE FUTURE—Drawn by Mr. Thomas Nast.—[See preceding Page.]

The KKK was a secret society that formed in 1865 after the end of the Civil War. It was a reaction to the **emancipation** of African Americans. The founding members believed in white supremacy, or the false idea that people with white skin are superior to other races. The KKK threatened and intimidated African Americans and other minority groups. They burned crosses and held marches and rallies. They carried out bombings, beatings, lynchings, and shootings, often in the dead of night, wearing the white hooded robes that hid their identities.

Unfortunately, the KKK is still an active hate group today. There is a movement underway to categorize the organization as a terrorist group. There are still chapters in 41 states across the country, but their size and power vary.

JAZZ IN THE 1930s

From the Novel

When Bud hears his grandfather's band practice, he is captivated by the sounds of the various instruments and the way they blend together. Miss Thomas begins to **scat**, and the addition of her voice to the music makes Bud fall in love with jazz.

Jazz began in New Orleans around 1915. Its roots were a combination of gospel music and European and African rhythms. A key element is **improvisation**, which means that the songs vary with every performance. By the 1920s, the "Jazz Age" was gaining popularity across the country. Jazz was often played by African American bands, with some neighborhoods like Harlem, New York, becoming famous for their jazz culture. Sadly, it was common for African Americans to be prohibited from listening to music in the same venues as whites.

Bee Bop a Diddly Wop Doo

Scat singing is a way of using the voice as a musical instrument. Sounds and syllables combine to create a vocal that adds spice to a song. It is said that Louis Armstrong was the first to scat, making a series of nonsense sounds after he dropped his sheet music. For some great examples of the masters scatting, listen to Louis Armstrong's "Ain't Misbehavin'," Ella Fitzgerald's "How High the Moon," and Sarah Vaughan's "Sassy's Blues."

Duke Ellington

Benny Goodman & Steve Allen

One of the great attractions of jazz during the Depression was that it made people forget their troubles. It was entertainment, it was fast-moving, and it was hard to think about anything else when you were dancing to it.

Some of the jazz greats at the time were Count Basie (pianist), Duke Ellington (composer and pianist), Ella Fitzgerald (vocalist), Benny Goodman (clarinetist), and Louis Armstrong (trumpeter). The music they popularized during one of America's hardest periods had lasting power. It was an escape for people at the time, but it still captures audiences today, nearly a century later.

First Lady of Song

Ella Fitzgerald remains one of the most popular female jazz singers of all time. She sold more than 40 million albums and was the recipient of 13 Grammy Awards in her lifetime. The "First Lady of Song" worked with all the jazz greats and captivated audiences worldwide. Fitzgerald was known for singing everything from sultry ballads to cheerful, bubbly jazz hits, as well as her amazing ability to imitate the sounds of instruments with her voice.

PULLMAN PORTERS

From the Novel

Mrs. Sleet tells Bud that her husband is a redcap, or **Pullman porter**. His daughter, Kim, proudly adds that he gets to travel all over the country for free. Although being a porter wasn't easy, it's clear that they saw prestige in having one in the family.

Between 1870 and 1969, *Pullman* was a well-known name. Pullman sleeping cars were attached to trains. They were not owned by the railroad company but served as a sort of moving hotel for customers traveling longer distances. Pullman cars could sleep approximately 150,000 passengers per night worldwide, and those passengers expected top-notch service and care.

End of an Era

By the late 1940s, train travel was on the decline. Interstate highways made car travel more popular, and flying was becoming an option. A company called Amtrak took over most passenger routes. The 1990s saw the retirement of the last of the original porters. If you're interested in learning more about this interesting piece of history, check out A Long Hard Journey: The Story of the Pullman Porter *by Patricia and Fredrick McKissack.*

Pullman Palace Sleeping Car. (Interior)

POSTAL TELEGRAPH   COMMERCIAL CABLES

TELEGRAM

transmits and delivers this message subject to the terms and conditions printed on the back of this blank.

Telegraph-Cable	TIME FILED.	CHECK.
COUNTER NUMBER.	Am	BAILEY MONET
013	12:32	

read the following message, without repeating, subject to the terms and conditions printed on the back hereof, which are hereby agreed to.

GRAND RAPIDS, MICHIGAN = SEPT 20 1936

MICHELLE RUTSHILLING STOP

MEETING RESCHEDULED STOP

NEW MEETING FOR DEC 10 AT 4:30PM STOP

LOOKING FORWARD TO SPEAKING STOP

JOSHUA JANES STOP

Porters did everything from making beds to shining shoes to sending and receiving telegrams. Although it was a desirable job to have, it was exhausting. Porters sometimes got only three hours of sleep per night. Most Pullman porters were African American. This was because racism supported the wrong idea that Black people should serve white people.

Pullman porters had a pivotal role in the Civil Rights Movement. In 1925, to help protect their rights, the African American employees of the Pullman Company organized a **labor union** called The Brotherhood of Sleeping Car Porters (BSCP). The BSCP fought many battles for the fair treatment and advancement of the Black community till 1978, when they merged with another union.

Dig Deeper

The BSCP wasn't just interested in advocating for Pullman porters. The leaders of the BSCP were vocal activists during the Civil Rights Movement. E.D. Nixon, who led the Montgomery Bus Boycott, was also a leader of the BSCP! If you want to know more about the rich history of BSCP's activism, go to Blackpast.org *and search the union's name.*

PROPERTY OWNERSHIP

From the Novel

Dirty Deed, one of Herman E. Calloway's band members, is white, while the other members are Black. Deed tells Bud that one of his roles in the band is to let Herman use his name. African Americans weren't allowed to own property in the area where the Log Cabin is located, so the club had to be in Deed's name.

In the early thirties, Americans were facing a housing shortage. The government's response to this was to create new housing programs that provided suburban housing to middle- and lower-class white people. Urban housing projects were left for African Americans and other people of color.

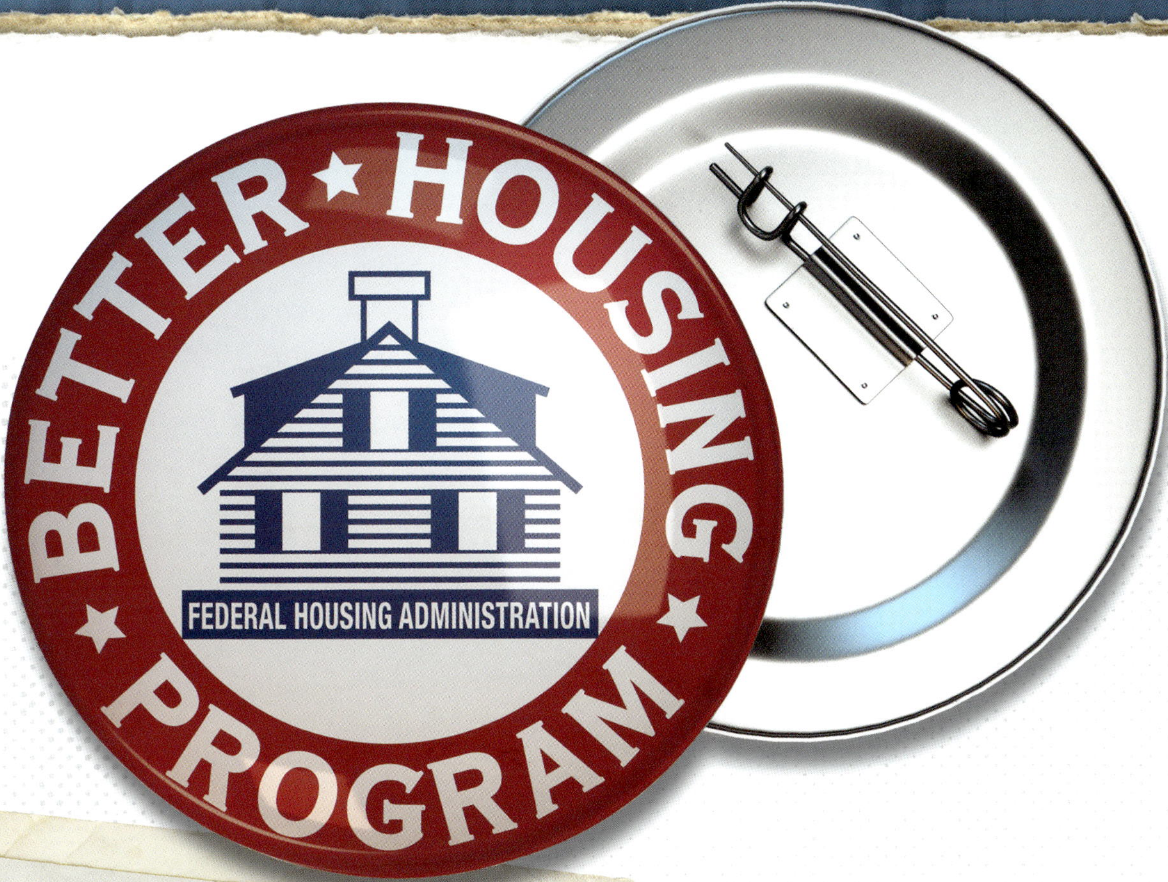
BETTER ★ HOUSING
FEDERAL HOUSING ADMINISTRATION
★ PROGRAM ★

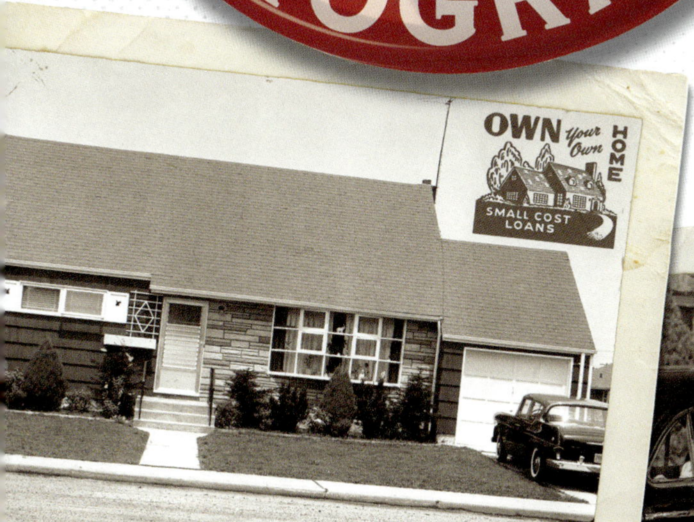
OWN Your Own HOME
SMALL COST LOANS

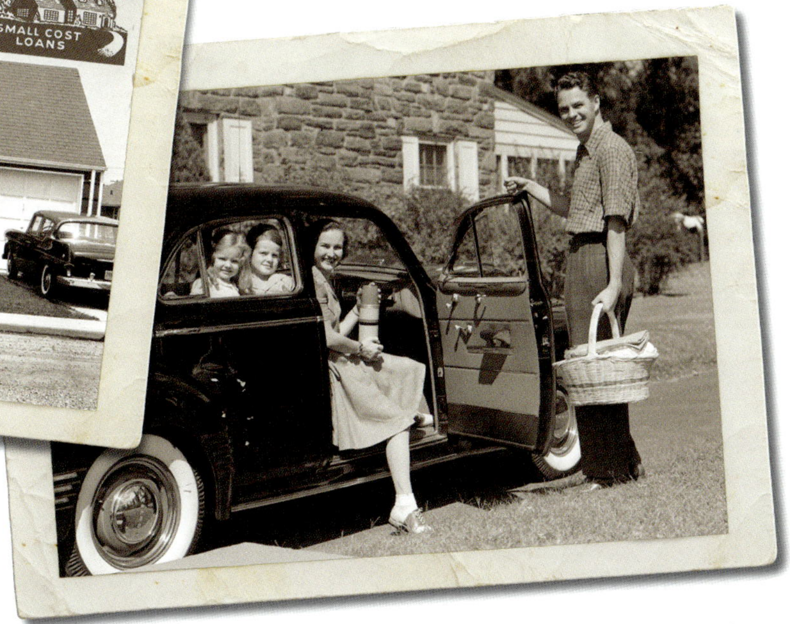

Maps were created that separated cities into four different categories. Areas made up primarily of minorities were highlighted in red, which gave rise to the expression **redlining**. Mortgage lenders were much less likely to issue loans to people in these areas or even in neighborhoods that were nearby. A single Black-owned house in the middle of a white neighborhood could make lenders wary.

Because African Americans could not get **mortgages** from mainstream lenders, they often had to rely on questionable lenders who charged higher interest rates or made unethical demands.

It was grossly unfair to people of color at the time, and the effects of this segregation still linger today.

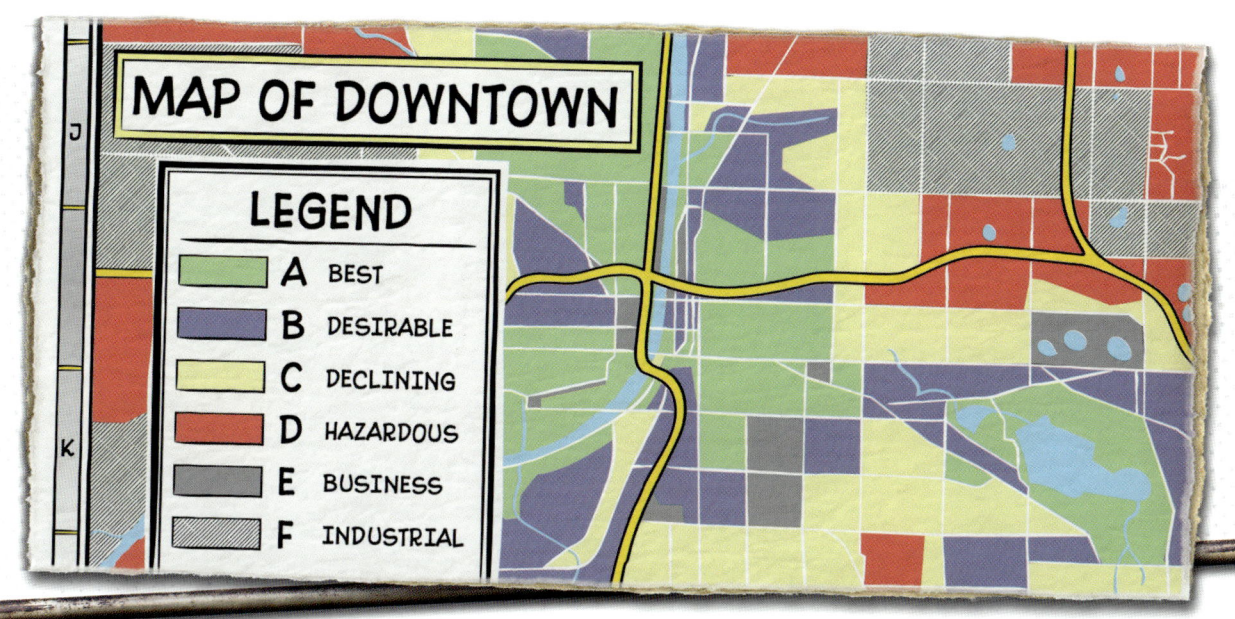

MAP OF DOWNTOWN

LEGEND

	A	BEST
	B	DESIRABLE
	C	DECLINING
	D	HAZARDOUS
	E	BUSINESS
	F	INDUSTRIAL

J

K

TELEGRAMS

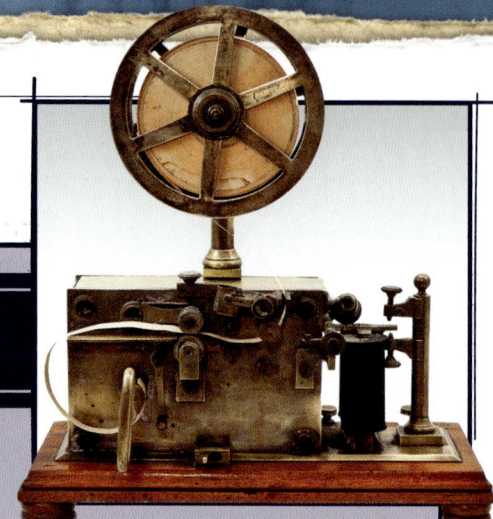

From the Novel

Lefty Lewis sends a telegram to Herman E. Calloway to let him know his "son" is safe, and he's bringing him back to Grand Rapids. When he shows Bud the return message, Bud has a hard time understanding the abbreviated wording.

Form No. 168.

THE WESTERN UNION TELEGRAPH COMPANY.

INCORPORATED

23,000 OFFICES IN AMERICA.   CABLE SERVICE TO ALL THE WORLD.

This Company TRANSMITS and DELIVERS messages only o.. conditions limiting its liability, which have been assented to by the sender of the following message. Errors can be guarded against only by repeating a message back to the sending station for comparison, and the Company will not hold itself liable for errors or delays in transmission or delivery of Unrepeated Messages, beyond the amount of tolls paid thereon, nor in any case where the claim is not presented in writing within sixty days after the message is filed with the Company for transmission.
This is an UNREPEATED MESSAGE, and is delivered by request of the sender, under the conditions named above.
ROBERT C. CLOWRY, President and General Manager.

RECEIVED at

86 B MI CS 33 PAID.   VIA FLINT MI

GRAND RAPIDS MI NOV 8

HEC STOP

BUD OK IN FLINT STOP

AT 4309 NORTH ST

STOP RETURN 8PM WED STOP

LEFTY STOP - 348P

Telegrams were a way to transmit messages quickly before phones were widely used. There were telegraph wires all over the U.S. The sender would transmit the message using **Morse code**. The receiver at the other end would write down the message, translate it, and give it to the recipient. The last telegraph was sent in 2006.

LABOR ORGANIZATIONS AND UNIONS

From the Novel

Lefty Lewis goes all the way to Flint to pick up flyers. The flyers can't be printed in Grand Rapids because they advertise a meeting to organize a union for Pullman porters.

Labor unions are groups of people organized by trade. Their goal is to protect the workers and stand up for their rights. They fight for better safety conditions, higher wages, reasonable hours, and so on. In general, employers are not supportive of unions. During the first five years of the Depression, companies pressured their employees not to form unions, including threatening them with lockouts and **blacklisting**.

In 1936 and 1937, labor unions in Flint, Michigan, organized sit-down strikes at the factory where Christopher Paul Curtis later worked. The workers sat down on the job so that the factory could not replace them.

The National Guard was brought in to remove the strikers, but luckily an agreement was reached before they had to use force. Curtis planned to write a book primarily about these strikes, but his writing took a different turn, and the book turned into *Bud, Not Buddy*.

DISCUSSION QUESTIONS

1. Describe several reasons someone might have chosen to ride the rails despite the risks.

2. Why did redlining make life more difficult for African Americans?

3. How was the Civil War linked to the founding of the KKK?

4. Why do you think employers tend not to be supportive of labor unions?

5. What were Hooverisms? Were they positive or negative? Why?

6. How is scatting different than singing?

7. Why was being a Pullman porter considered a good job, even though the hours were long and the work exhausting?

Dizzy Gillespie

WRITING PROMPTS AND PROJECTS

1. In 2008, the U.S. suffered an economic crisis that had many similarities to the Great Depression. Do some research and explain what the two crises had in common and how they were different.

2. Search online or at the library to see if you can find a redlining map of your city or a nearby city. Are the areas on the map that were least or most desirable at the time still the same?

3. The author used many sources to write this book. One of those is a free website called *blackpast.org* and it has many articles about Black history! Go to *blackpast.org* and search for articles about African American history during the Great Depression.
Find an article that interests you, then write a paragraph on why you chose that article and what you learned after reading it.

4. Do some research to find tips on frugal, or inexpensive, living from the Great Depression.

   - Make a booklet, brochure, or poster with your favorites. You can create it on a computer or by hand. Include illustrations, either hand-drawn or found online.

   - Try at least two of the tips and add your testimony about their effectiveness to your project.

   - Present your project to friends or family, or take some photos and e-mail them to a faraway family member.

GLOSSARY

blacklisting (BLAK-listing): putting people on a list of disapproval, generally to punish them or block them from employment

emancipation (ih-man-suh-PAY-shun): the act of setting someone, or a group of people, free

Hooverville (HOO-ver-vil): a grouping of temporary shelters, often on the edge of a town, where homeless and unemployed people resided during the Depression

improvisation (im-prov-uh-ZAY-shun): the act of performing or playing an instrument without preparing beforehand or following a plan

labor unions (LAY-ber YOON-yuns): groups of workers organized by trade with the purpose of protecting the workers

mortgages (MAWR-gijz): loans for the purpose of owning property

Morse code (mawrs code): a system of dots and dashes or short and long sounds used for communication

Pullman porter (PUHL-mun PAWR-ter): an attendant who worked on a railroad passenger car

redlining (RED-line-ing): the discriminatory act of refusing to loan money to borrowers who live within certain geographical areas

Roaring Twenties (RAWR-ing TWEN-tees): nickname for the prosperous period of the 1920s, right before the Great Depression

scat (skat): to sing using nonsense syllables and sounds rather than words

stock market (stok MAHR-kit): a place where people can buy and sell partial ownership in companies

BIBLIOGRAPHY

Curtis, Christopher Paul. *Bud, Not Buddy*. New York: Yearling, 1999.

George, Enzo. *The Jazz Age and the Great Depression.*
New York: Brown Bear Books Ltd., 2016.

History.com Editors. "Hoovervilles." Last updated Nov. 2, 2018.
https://www.history.com/topics/great-depression/hoovervilles.

History.com Editors. "Ku Klux Klan." Last updated February 21, 2020.
https://www.history.com/topics/reconstruction/ku-klux-klan.

Mullenbach, Cheryl. *The Great Depression for Kids: Hardship and Hope in 1930s America with 21 Activities.*
Chicago: Chicago Review Press, 2015.

Museum of the American Railroad. "The Legacy of Pullman Porters." Accessed June 21, 2020.
http://www.museumoftheamericanrailroad.org/LearnTheLegacyofPullmanPorters.aspx.

NPR. "A 'Forgotten History' of How the U.S. Government Segregated America." May 3, 2017.
https://www.npr.org/2017/05/03/526655831/a-forgotten-history-of-how-the-u-s-government-segregated-america.

Salter, Daren. "The Brotherhood of Sleeping Car Porters (1925-1978)." Accessed Aug. 28, 2020.
www.blackpast.org/african-american-history/brotherhood-sleeping-car-porters-1925-1978/

Smithsonian Year of Music. Accessed June 3, 2020.
https://music.si.edu/spotlight/african-american-music/jazz-blues.

Zinn Education Project. "Aug. 25 1925: Brotherhood of Sleeping Car Porters." Accessed Aug. 28, 2020.
www.zinnedproject.org/news/tdih/sleeping-car-porters/

INDEX TERMS

ABOUT THE AUTHOR

Lisa Kurkov lives in Charlotte, North Carolina, where she and her husband homeschool their two children. When her head isn't buried in a book, Lisa enjoys baking, crafting, photography, birding, and adventuring with her family.

www.rourkeeducationalmedia.com

PHOTO CREDITS: page 1: Szasz-Fabian Jozsef/Shutterstock.com; page 4: alisafarov/Shutterstock.com; page 5: scanrail/Getty Images; page 5: scanrail/Getty Images; page 5: MBR/KRT/Newscom; page 6: lchumpitaz/Getty Images; page 7: Casarsa/Getty Images; page 8: BardoczPeter/Getty Images; page 8: digitalskillet/Getty Images; page 9: FrankRamspott/Getty Images; page 10: ratpack223/Getty Images; page 10: manley099/Getty Images; page 11: heidijpix/Getty Images; page 11: stacey_newman/Getty Images; page 11: subjug/Getty Images; page 11: Elias Goldensky/ZUMA Press/Newscom; page 12: dovate/Getty Images; page 12: Everett Collection/Newscom; page 13: Everett Collection/Newscom; page 13: Everett Collection/Newscom; page 14: Everett Collection/Newscom; page 14: Staff/Mirrorpix/Newscom; page 15: Everett Collection/Newscom; page 15: Underwood Archives/UIG Universal Images Group/Newscom; page 16: enviromantic/Getty Images; page 16: Historica Graphica Collection Heritage Images/Newscom; page 17: Picture History/Newscom; page 18: picturehistory004533; page 19: Everett Collection/Newscom; page 20: olaser/Getty Images; page 20: JennaWagner/Getty Images; page 20: akg-images/Newscom; page 21: a-poselenov; page 21: subjug/Getty Images; page 21: Igor Sokolov/Getty Images; page Everett Collection/Shutterstock.com; page 22: Zenobillis/Getty Images; page 22: Glasshouse Images Glasshouse Images/Newscom; page 22: James W. Prichard/ZUMAPRESS/Newscom; page 24: Thomas Nast/Heritage Art/Heritage Images AiWire/Newscom; page 26: JT Vintage/ZUMA Press/Newscom; page 27 Punnarong/Getty Images; page 27: Stx_Stefan/Shutterstock.com; page 27: AiWire/Newscom; page 28: Tolga TEZCAN/Getty Images; page 28: AiWire/Newscom; page 28: Universal Images Group/Newscom; page 29: itKEYSTONE Pictures USA/ZUMAPRESS/Newscom; page 30: subjug/Getty Images; page 30: Everett Collection/Newscom; page 31: Tim Shaffer/REUTERS/Newscom; page 31: World History Archive/Newscom; page 32: jmbatt/Getty Images; page 32: Everett Collection/Newscom; page 32: Liszt Collection/Newscom; page 33: Everett Collection/Newscom; page 33: Everett Collection/Newscom; page 34: Lorado/Getty Images; page 34: World History Archive/Newscom; page 35: gazanfer/Getty Images; page 35: George Marks/Getty Images; page 35: H. Armstrong Roberts/Getty Images; page 35: RetroClipArt/ Shutterstock.com; page 36: Underwood Archives/UIG Universal Images Group/Newscom; page 37: World History Archive/Newscom; page 38: unser/Getty Images; page 38: Picture History/Newscom; page 39: jayfish/Getty Images; page 39: World History Archive/Newscom; page 40: Everett Collection/Newscom; page 41: Everett Collection/Newscom; page 42: Everett Collection/Newscom; page 44: JT Vintage/ZUMA Press/Newscom; cover: Igor Sokolov/ Getty Images; cover: natthanim/ Getty Images; cover: Tolga TEZCAN/ Getty Images; cover: Casarsa/ Getty Images; cover: JonGorr/ Getty Images; cover: digitalskillet/ Getty Images; cover: Picture History/Newscom; page n/a: enjoynz/ Getty Images; page n/a: -slav-/ Getty Images

Library of Congress PCN Data

Nonfiction Companion to Christopher Paul Curtis's Bud, Not Buddy / Lisa Kurkov
(Nonfiction Companions)
ISBN 9781-7-3164-340-7 (hard cover)
ISBN 9781-7-3164-304-9 (soft cover)
ISBN 9781-7-3164-372-8 (e-Book)
ISBN 9781-7-3164-436-7 (epub)
Library of Congress Control Number: 2020945081

Rourke Educational Media
Printed in the United States of America
01-3502011937

Edited by: Madison Capitano
Cover and interior design by: Joshua Janes